FOREWORD

Wigan has an extraordinary history which has been enriched and expanded by recent archaeological investigations, especially those relating to the town's Roman origins. The Greater Manchester Archaeological Unit's excavations near The Wiend in the early 1980s demonstrated several phases of Roman activity; Wigan Archaeological Society's work has shown that Wigan was a focal point for the Roman road network; and finally, Oxford Archaeology North's investigations ahead of the Grand Arcade and Joint Service Centre developments have proved that, without doubt, Wigan was a significant Roman site in the late first and second centuries AD. This remarkable story of discovery is revealed in this booklet, which is a precursor to the publication of a more detailed account of Wigan's archaeological investigations.

CO

Introduction........................3
Wigan's Early History........................8
The First Evidence for Roman Wigan 12
The Question of *Coccium* 14
The Roman Roads 15
Excavations in Roman Wigan 22
The Finds 36
Finding Roman Wigan 38
The Planning Background........................42
Glossary 44
Further Reading 45
Acknowledgements........................46

Archaeology has a wonderful way of springing surprises; despite best guesses, you never know what might be uncovered digging down through the layers of soil. To discover the complete plan of a substantial Roman baths complex, set back from modern Millgate, was astonishing. Originally a impressive stone building, the baths were dismantled and the materials removed so that it passed out of local memory. Yet, by an amazing coincidence, its hidden remains lay only a stone's throw from the modern swimming baths!

'Roman Wigan' is Volume 3 in new series called *Greater Manchester's Past Revealed*, covering not only Wigan's wonderful archaeology, but also that of the whole of the Greater Manchester area. It provides a format for publishing significant archaeology from developer-funded, research or community projects in an attractive, easy to read style. This booklet is a tribute to the archaeologists whose painstaking work has uncovered the remarkable evidence for Wigan's Roman origins, and to the planning system and support of Wigan Council and developers, that allowed the archaeological remains to be fully recorded.

NORMAN REDHEAD, County Archaeologist, Greater Manchester

INTRODUCTION

Aerial view across Wigan, looking north-east towards the Pennines (© webbaviation)

The metropolitan borough of Wigan covers an area of some 200km², forming the north-western part of Greater Manchester, and has a border with Lancashire, Warrington and Merseyside. Wigan is the principal town in this large borough, which also includes Leigh, Ashton-in-Makerfield, Tyldesley, Hindley and Standish. It is renowned as one of the key industrial towns of nineteenth-century Lancashire, with a vibrant economy that was based largely on coal, cotton and iron. This is reflected in the wealth of industrial buildings that survive, such as the impressive Trencherfield and Swan Meadow cotton mills, which together line the historic Leeds and Liverpool Canal as it loops around the southern edge of the town. Some of the fine public buildings that grace the town centre, many dating from the late Victorian and early Edwardian years, similarly derive from the prosperity brought by Wigan's strong industrial base.

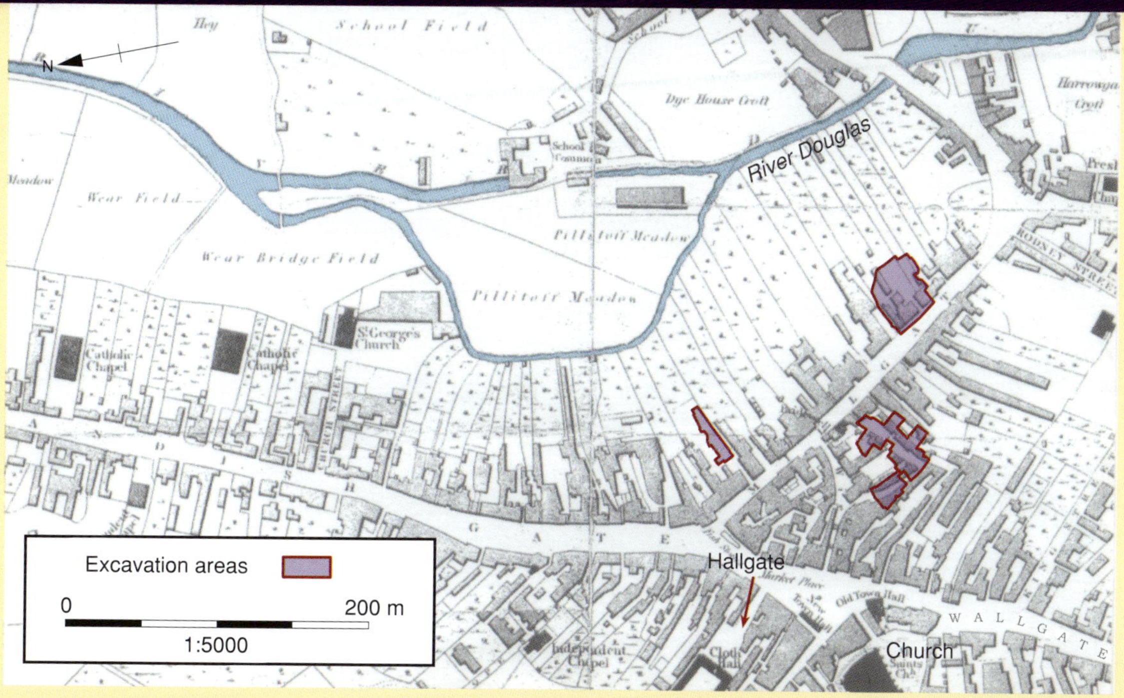

Extract from Mather's Plan of Wigan *of 1827, on which can be seen the main elements of the medieval town*

Physical reminders of Wigan's prowess as one of only four boroughs in historical Lancashire to possess a Royal Charter are less obvious, although Wallgate, Standishgate and Hallgate still represent the layout of the medieval town. The junction of these principal thoroughfares at the Market Place marks the centre of the town, which is overlooked by the parish church. The Wiend and Millgate, leading south-eastwards from the Market Place to a bridge across the River Douglas, were also important elements of the medieval settlement.

The origins of a settlement at Wigan are considerably earlier, however, and there is compelling evidence to show that the Roman army had occupied the area before the end of the first century AD. This was realised initially in the nineteenth century, when numerous

View of the archaeological excavation on the site of the Grand Arcade in 2005

Roman artefacts were discovered during construction work across the town. In particular, the remains of a cemetery were identified, providing good evidence for there having been a Roman settlement at Wigan. However, very little was known about this settlement until recent archaeological excavations along Millgate showed conclusively that Wigan has a very important Roman heritage.

Remarkable foundations of a prestigious Roman building were discovered during a large excavation on the site of the Grand Arcade Shopping Development in 2004-5. The remains of smaller Roman buildings were also recorded on the opposite side of Millgate, close to the junction with The Wiend, during excavations directed by the Greater Manchester Archaeological Unit (GMAU) in the 1980s. Further excavation of this site was carried out in 2008, prior to the construction of the Joint Service Centre, providing more fascinating evidence for Roman Wigan.

This booklet aims to present the new and exciting findings from these archaeological excavations. Whilst these have also produced a fresh insight into the development of the town from the medieval period onwards, the Roman remains were of especial importance, and it is this early chapter in Wigan's long history that is summarised here. A comprehensive account of the excavations, presenting the archaeological evidence for all stages in the development of the town, is also being produced. An attempt has been made here to provide an interpretation of Roman Wigan, although it should be borne in mind that this is based on the evidence that is currently available, and will be refined in the light of discoveries from any future excavations.

The Natural Setting

The modern landscape of the borough has taken thousands of years to evolve, although dramatic urban and industrial expansion during the nineteenth and twentieth centuries wrought the greatest changes. Topographically, Wigan occupies low-lying land known as the Makerfield Basin, which is enclosed to the north and east by the raised plateau of Central Lancashire and the West Pennine Moors. Conversely, to the west, the ground level falls sharply down to the West Lancashire Plain, whilst the natural topography to the south-east is dominated by the extensive wetland of Chat Moss.

Whilst much of the region would have been populated only sparsely, some large settlements developed following the initial Roman occupation of the North West in the AD 70s. The most important centre in the region was the legionary fortress at Chester, although small towns also evolved around other Roman forts, such as those at Manchester, Northwich, Ribchester and Lancaster. Industrial settlements were also established at Wilderspool and Walton-le-Dale, which lay at important fording points of the rivers Mersey and Ribble respectively.

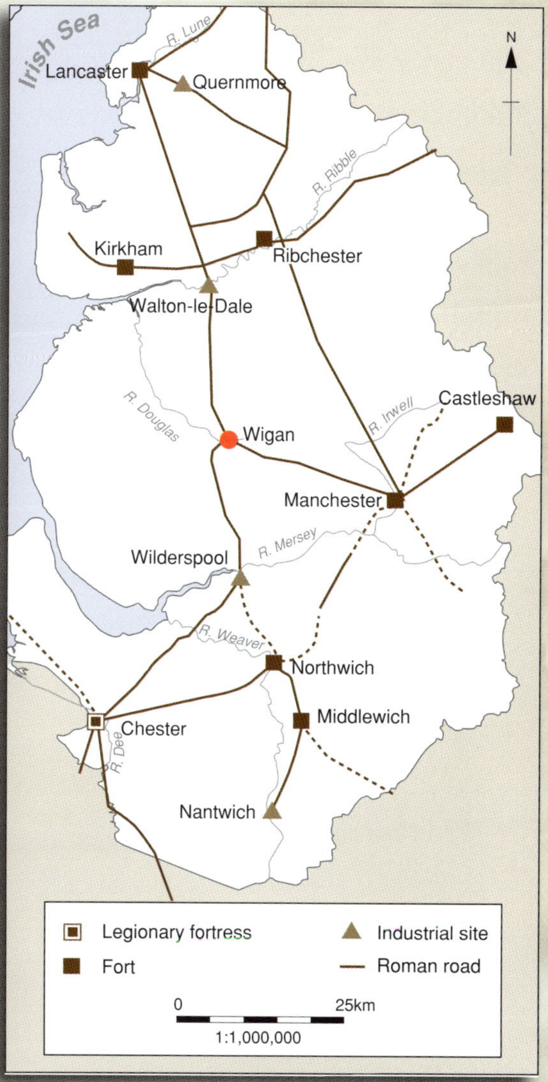

Map of the Roman North West, showing the key military sites

Wigan lay approximately midway between these two settlements, and is likely to have been a valuable resting point for anyone travelling along the main north/south route. It may also have been an important crossing point of the River Douglas, although a ford has yet to be identified.

The historic core of Wigan lies atop a small hill that rises from the valley of the River Douglas, although the advantage of this elevated position is today masked by the density of buildings that form the town centre. Similarly, the canalised course of the River Douglas, which takes a broad loop around the eastern and southern sides of the town, is largely hidden from view today by modern development. The river used to incorporate a wide meander that cut into the hill upon which the town stands, but this was filled in and the ground level on the western bank was raised by several metres to allow the Central Station to be built in 1892. The natural topography has been altered further by modern schemes, such as the Riverway dual carriageway (A49) and the Grand Arcade Shopping Development, which have subsumed the natural steep slope on the western side of the river.

View looking up Millgate, showing the Grand Arcade built into the natural slope

WIGAN'S EARLY HISTORY

The spur of high ground overlooking the River Douglas may have been an attractive location for prehistoric settlement, although there is very little evidence to show that this strategic site was occupied before the Roman period. Indeed, firm evidence for prehistoric activity across the entire borough is dependent largely on a few artefacts discovered by chance.

The earliest of these finds probably date to the Neolithic period (*c* 4000 – 2200 BC), and include polished stone axes that were reported as discoveries at Bickershaw Hall in 1831, at Leigh cricket ground in 1912, and at Boar's Head railway station near Standish in 1928. Closer to the centre of Wigan, a stone axe was found at Bottling Wood in 1911, and another example was unearthed in 1933 during construction work on Walkden Avenue, near Mesnes Park. Flint tools are also known from the area, including a small flint scraper that was discovered at a garden in Winstanley and, more recently, three small flint flakes that were recovered from the archaeological excavations on Millgate in 2008.

Two polished stone axes, one thought to have been found at Leigh in 1912 (top), the other thought to have been found at Boar's Head in 1928 (bottom) (both images courtesy of Wigan Heritage Services)

Flint flakes from excavations on Millgate

Boar's Den Bronze Age round barrow, Wrightington

Little is known about the lifestyle of the people who made these tools, although it is likely that they led a nomadic existence as hunter-gatherers. The Wigan area would have been part of the territory of one or more of these groups, who lived by exploiting the natural resources of what would have been a largely forested area.

The earliest indication of more permanent settlement dates to the Bronze Age (*c* 2300 - *c* 700 BC), when small farming communities became established across the North West. The most visible remains from this period are funerary monuments known as round barrows, such as Boar's Den near Wrightington. Lying some 8.5km to the north-west of Wigan, this earth and stone mound measures 64m in diameter and is some 2.5m high. Another well-known round barrow lies at Winwick, some 16km to the south of Wigan, where excavation in 1860 yielded a large urn containing human bones, a stone axe hammer and a bronze spear head. Both of these sites are protected as Scheduled Monuments, reflecting their national importance.

Other rare evidence for prehistoric settlement in the area was discovered in 2007 during an archaeological excavation at the Cutacre opencast coal mine, close to the south-eastern boundary of the modern borough, where the remains of a roundhouse of probable Iron-Age date were identified. This consisted of a ring of postholes forming a structure that was approximately 7m in diameter, with an entrance to the south-east. Traces of a smaller rectangular structure were also identified, together with a few fragments of pottery and charred plant material. Few roundhouses have been identified in the North West, but that at Cutacre appeared to be of a similar form and size to those excavated at Duttons Farm in Lathom, Great Woolden Hall near Cadishead in Salford, and at Mellor near Stockport.

Iron Age roundhouse reconstructed at Orrell as part of a community-based project in the late 1980s (courtesy of GMAU)

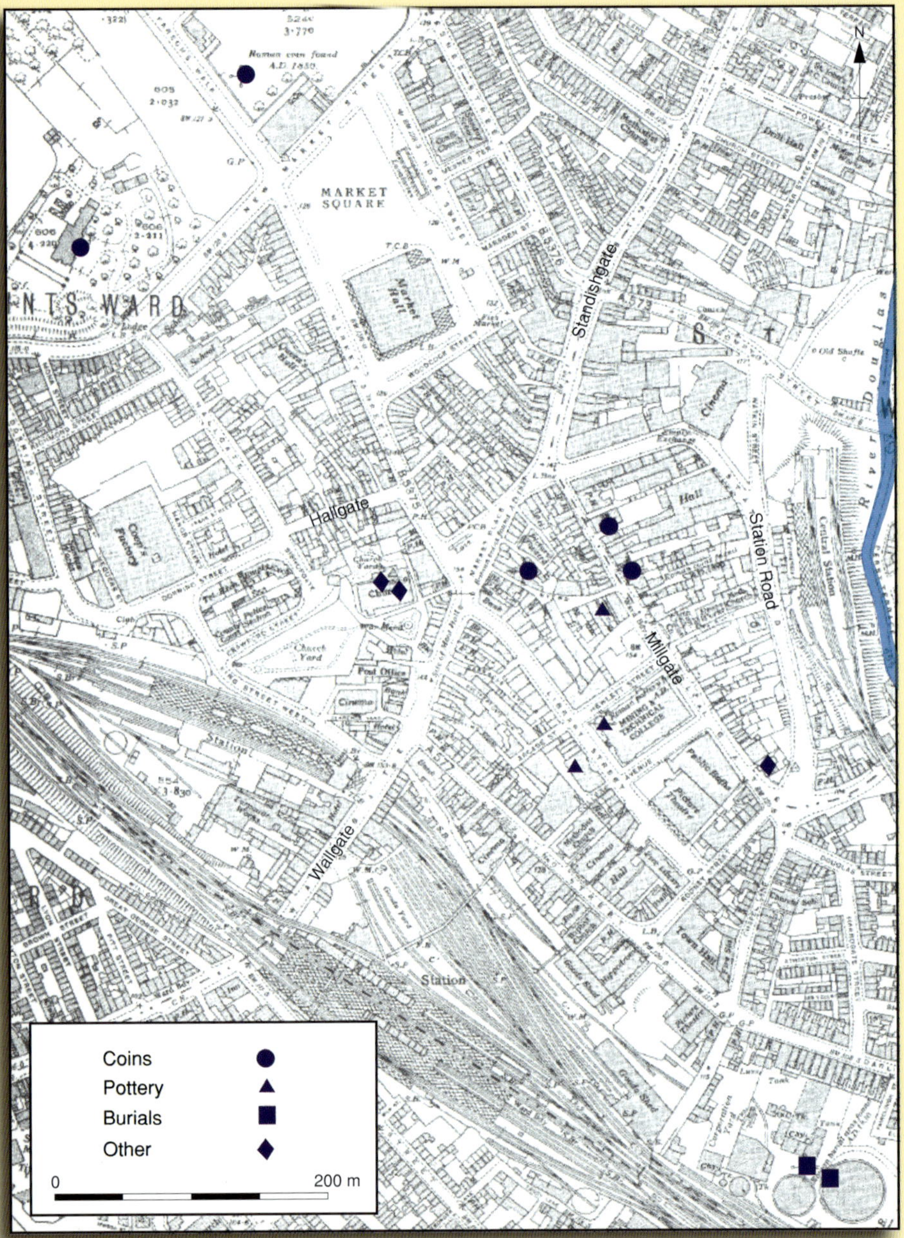

Nineteenth-century findspots of Roman artefacts and features in Wigan, superimposed on the Ordnance Survey map of 1939

THE FIRST EVIDENCE FOR ROMAN WIGAN

The first signs of Wigan's Roman past were provided by antiquarian observations during the construction of the gas works to the south of Darlington Street between 1822 and 1830. There, numerous fragments of Roman urns were discovered, together with thick deposits of charcoal and fragments of burnt bone, implying that the area had been used as a cemetery. Some evidence for an associated settlement was derived from chance finds of coins and pottery during building works across the town in the nineteenth century, with a particular concentration coming from the Library Street and Millgate area, suggesting that Roman activity had been focused on the summit of the hill.

Above: Aureus of Vitellius
Below: Roman coins found at the Boar's Head in 1926 (courtesy of Wigan Heritage Services)

An important find was a gold coin, known as an aureus, that was found somewhere on The Mesnes in 1850. This coin was issued during the reign of Vitellius, who was emperor for just eight months in AD 69, and its discovery may imply that there had been some Roman activity in Wigan as early as that date.

Other coins from the town include a group with a date range spanning the late second to late third centuries AD, found near the Market Place in 1837, and fourth-century coins unearthed at The Mesnes and at Wigan Rectory. Roman coins have also been discovered on the fringe of the town, including large hoards of silver coins that were discovered at Standish in the eighteenth century, and near Boar's Head in 1926.

An intriguing object of uncertain provenance is a large worked stone that is built into the wall of Wigan parish church. The stone is inscribed with the date 1604, although its size and shape closely resemble a Roman altar.

The worked stone in Wigan parish church that may originally have been a Roman altar

Another possible indication of Roman religious practice in the borough is a headless statue of Cautopates, which was reported as a discovery at Appley Bridge in 1932, although its exact provenance has been questioned. In Roman mythology, Cautopates and Cautes were torch-bearing attendants of the deity Mithras, the central figure of a mysterious religion that was practised widely, until it was harshly suppressed in the fourth century. The popularity of this religion is reflected in the number of Mithraic temples that have been found in the Roman empire, including the well-preserved example at Carrawburgh on Hadrian's Wall in Northumberland. Other images of Cautopates have also been discovered elsewhere in Britain, including an example that was found during construction work on Chester Road in Manchester in 1821.

Left: Statue of Cautopates reported as a discovery at Appley Bridge
Right: Mithraic stone relief found in Manchester in 1821

THE QUESTION OF *COCCIUM*

The chance finds in the town provided a clear indication that a Roman settlement had existed at Wigan, although its size, status and name remained unknown. One avenue of research to establish the name is a Roman document, known as the Antonine Itinerary, which is believed to have been compiled during the early third century. This is essentially a list of routes across the Roman Empire, giving the distances between named places through which these passed.

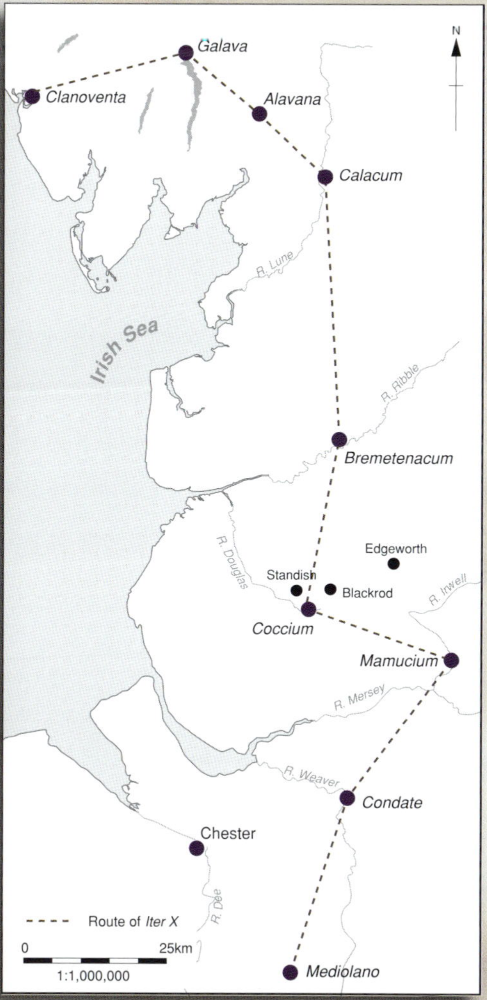

Roman sites listed in Iter X *of the Antonine Itinerary*

The Antonine Itinerary describes 15 routes within Roman Britain, of which the tenth (*Iter X*) is of relevance to Wigan. *Iter X* traces a route of 150 Roman miles from *Clanoventa*, which is thought to have been Ravenglass on the Cumbrian coast, to *Mediolano*, normally held to be Whitchurch, in Shropshire. Seven places are named on this route, including *Bremetenacum* (Ribchester), and *Mamucium* (Manchester). The post between these two Roman forts, said to have been situated 20 Roman miles from the former and 17 miles from the latter, is named as *Coccium*, the exact location of which has been debated for centuries. It was not until the nineteenth century that the name *Coccium* was linked to Wigan, although other places, including Blackrod, Edgeworth and even Standish, have been proposed as alternatives. However, the important remains exposed by the recent archaeological excavations on Millgate have shown beyond reasonable doubt that Wigan was a Roman settlement of considerable importance, and is thus almost certainly the site of *Coccium*.

THE ROMAN ROADS

Another important factor in firmly establishing the town's identification as *Coccium* is Wigan's relationship to the network of Roman roads across the region. The main roads were almost certainly surveyed and laid out by the Roman army during the military conquest of Britain in the first century AD. These were essential lines of communication between Roman forts, and were crucial for effective government and trading. Many roads were laid upon a well-constructed embankment, called an *agger*, which provided a properly drained base that was essential to the maintenance of the road. The material for the *agger* was often derived from the excavation of a ditch along one or both sides of the road, and these also helped to drain surface water away. The roads were designed to withstand heavy traffic, and thus required a solid foundation that often comprised large stones. The foundation was typically overlain by layers of rammed gravel, small stones or flints, although the exact composition of the surfacing was dependent upon the materials that were available locally. The roads that crossed the Pennines, such as that between Manchester and the fort at Castleshaw, for instance, incorporated much more stone than was used in those around Wigan, creating a surface that was far more substantial and robust.

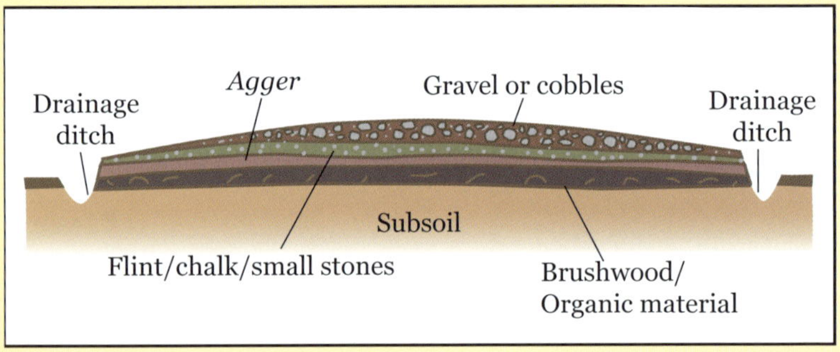

Idealised section of a Roman road

Geographically, Wigan is situated roughly midway between the Roman industrial settlements at Wilderspool and Walton-le-Dale, which were established on the principal north/south Roman road across north-west England. This route is thought to have been joined at Wigan by another road, which led eastwards to the Roman fort at Manchester.

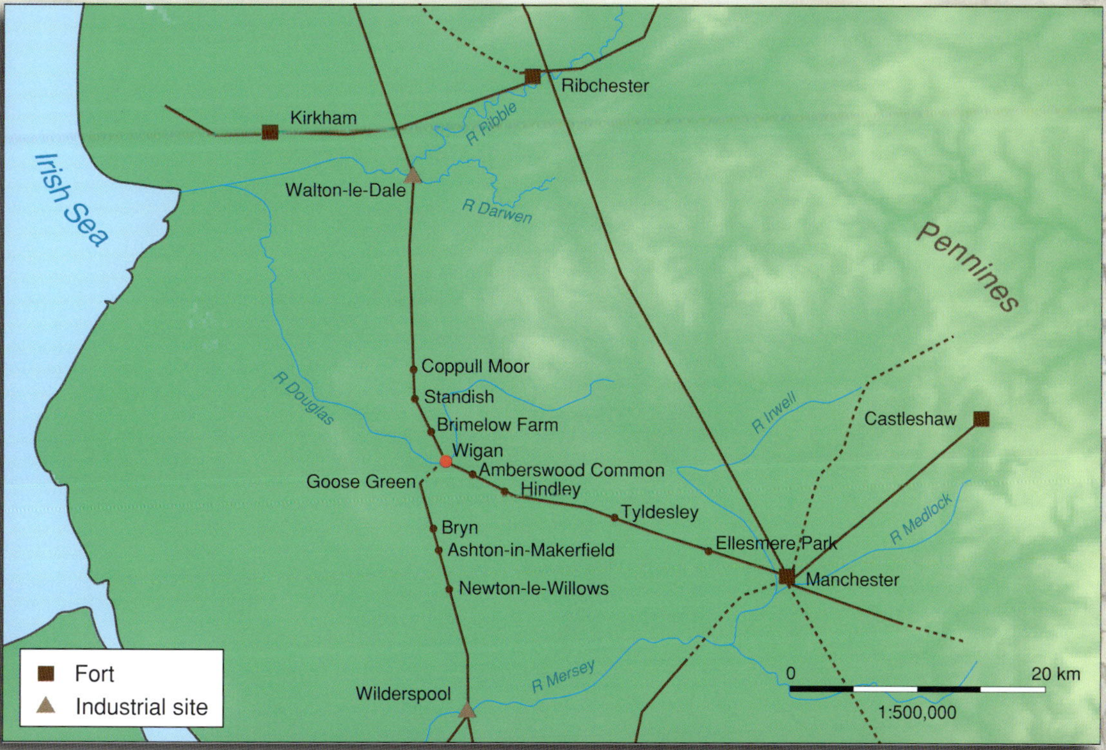

The main Roman roads in South Lancashire

The lines of these roads were traced in the 1830s by the Reverend Edmund Sibson, the minister of Ashton-in-Makerfield, who described their appearance and direction with reference to nearby landmarks. A similar approach was taken in the 1870s by W Thompson Watkin, who also wrote a detailed description of the Roman roads in the area, largely corroborating Sibson's account. More recently, establishing the routes described in these nineteenth-century accounts has been the objective of numerous archaeological investigations, which have attempted to identify the precise line of several sections of the Roman roads around Wigan, and have provided a record of the buried remains. Many of these investigations have been carried out by the Wigan Archaeological Society (WAS) as part of their Roman Roads Project, a continuous programme of works that was started in 1982.

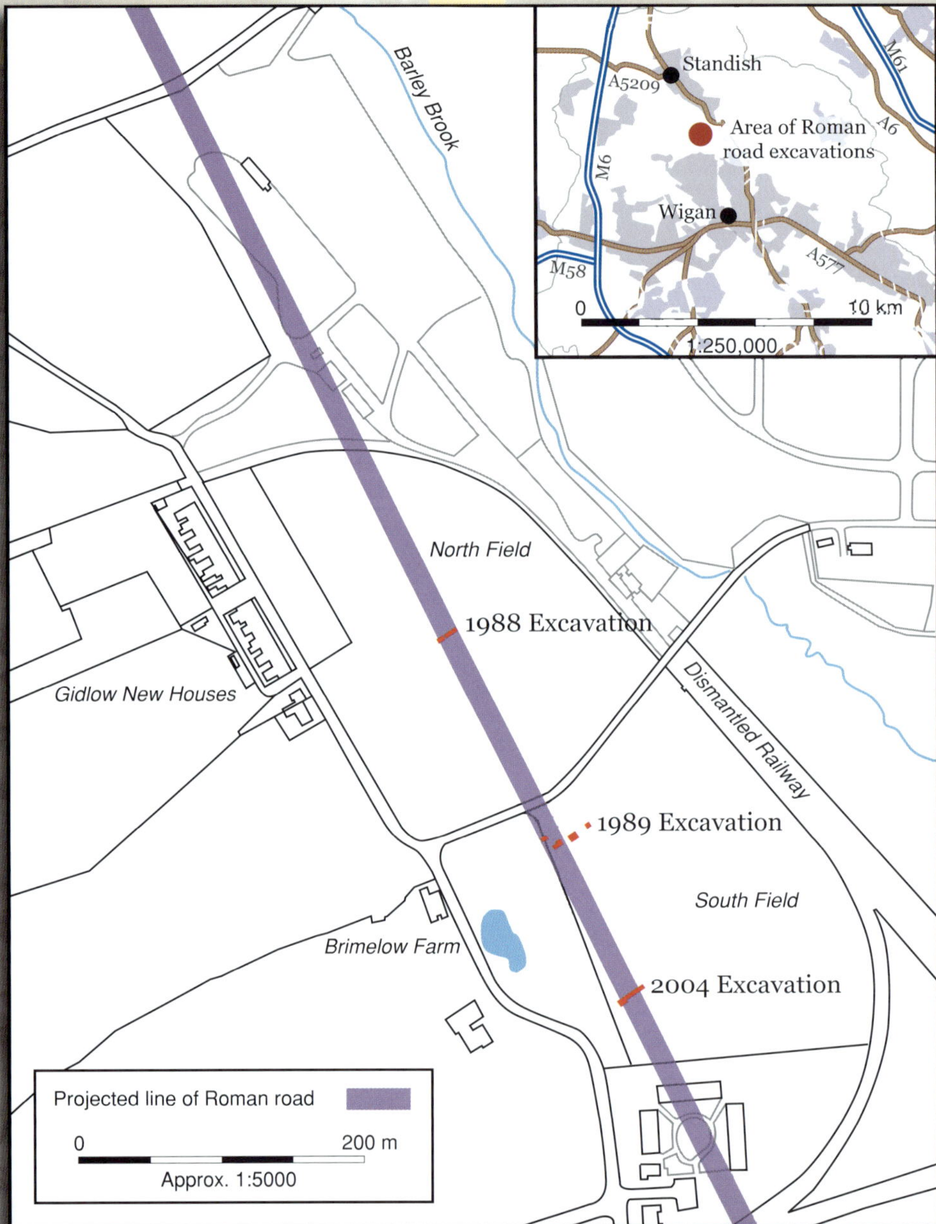

Projected line of the Roman road north of Wigan, showing the location of archaeological investigations carried out by Wigan Archaeological Society (courtesy of WAS)

North/South Route

The line of the Roman road between Wilderspool and Walton-le-Dale is difficult to trace in the modern landscape, although the stretch between Wilderspool and Wigan, passing through Newton-le-Willows and Ashton-in-Makerfield, is followed closely by the modern A49. A buried section of this road was unearthed at Bryn, some 5.5km to the south of Wigan, during an archaeological evaluation carried out by GMAU in 1993. The road was seen to be at least 5m wide, with a gently cambered profile. It was constructed using irregular-shaped blocks of sandstone, bedded onto a base of sand and gravel, although there was no surviving evidence for the metalled gravel surface that is often associated with Roman roads.

Section of the Roman road exposed at Bryn in 1993 (courtesy of GMAU)

Continuing northwards from Bryn, the line of the Roman road has been traced as far as Goose Green, which lies some 2.8km to the south-west of Wigan, after which the route is lost. It has been suggested that the road continued north to Standish, passing to the west of Wigan, although firm evidence is lacking. Conversely, a short section of a Roman road leading north out of Wigan towards Standish is marked on the Ordnance Survey 1": 1 mile map of 1842-4, taking a route described subsequently by W Thompson Watkin. The line of this road has been investigated on several occasions by WAS in the vicinity of Brimelow Farm, some 2km to the north of Wigan town centre.

A section of the cobbled surface excavated by WAS at Brimelow Farm in 2004 (courtesy of WAS)

At Brimelow Farm, attention was focused on two fields lying to the east of the farmhouse, where resistivity surveys were carried out in 1986 across the suspected line of the road. The results from the survey in the northern field were particularly encouraging, with high readings being obtained from an area in the centre of the field. In 1988, WAS excavated two narrow trenches across this area, and exposed a metalled surface with a shallow ditch along its western side. The surface was typical of a Roman road, measuring some 8m wide, and comprising a mixture of river-washed cobbles and flat blocks of sandstone in a matrix of smaller stones, sand and compacted gravel.

Further resistivity surveys using more sophisticated equipment were carried out in 2004, and a short trench was excavated across the southern field. This revealed a continuation of the metalled surface, which was again seen to be approximately 8m wide, and almost certainly represented the remains of the Roman road.

From Brimelow Farm, the line of the road continues north-north-west for about 3km to Prospect Hill, near Standish, where it probably turns northwards. The road may also have been exposed at the junction of Coppull Moor Lane and Hic Bibi Lane, some 5km to the north of Standish, where a metalled surface was excavated by the Chorley Archaeological Society in 1959, and again in 1985.

The Route from Wigan to Manchester

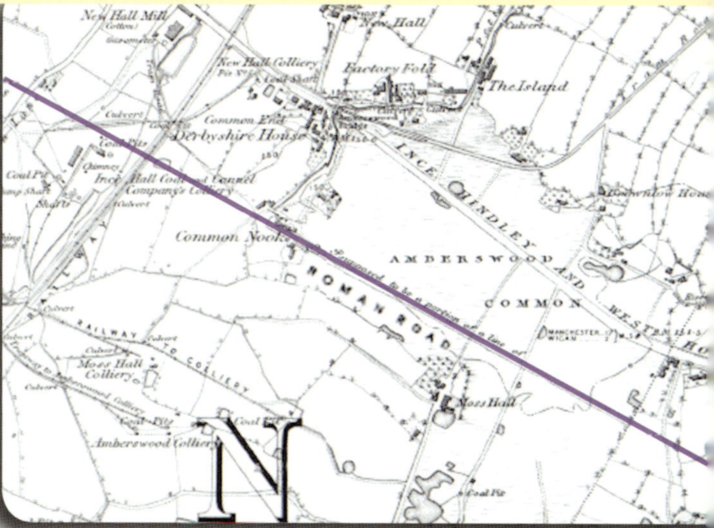

Extract from the Ordnance Survey map of 1849, marking the line of the Roman road across Amberswood Common

The Roman road between Manchester and Wigan is thought to have taken broadly the same course as the modern A577. A section of this route is marked on the Ordnance Survey 6": 1 mile map of 1849, which shows the road taking a course across Amberswood Common, between Ince and Hindley. This is where the Reverend Sibson had claimed that its line was 'very visible'.

In 2003, members of WAS, with support from Wigan Council, excavated three trenches near Amberswood Common in Higher Ince, as part of Channel 4's Big Dig project. A bank of clay was exposed in each trench, which could be interpreted as the foundation for the road. The bank was approximately 11m wide and, in places, incorporated a distinct camber. A spread of large cobbles was exposed in one of the trenches, which seemed to be acting as a revetment for the clay bank on the south side.

A continuation of the road was excavated by GMAU near Atherton Road at Hindley in 1995. There, the road was identified with a maximum width of 8.2m, and a structural depth of up to 200mm.

The trench excavated at Amberswood Common (courtesy of WAS)

Another section of this road was investigated at the Three Sisters in Ellesmere Park estate near Eccles in 2005, by the Ellesmere Park Residents Association working in conjunction with WAS. In the first instance, WAS carried out a series of resistivity surveys at three locations in the estate, and obtained particularly good readings that corresponded to the projected line of the road there. The results were tested by excavating a narrow trench, which exposed a well-preserved section of a metalled surface composed of cobbles and rammed gravel. The surface was approximately 6m wide, with well-defined ditches on both sides. A layer of organic material was identified at the base of the road, suggesting that it had been laid upon a foundation of brushwood. Lenses of organic material deriving from buried turf have been found preserved beneath Roman roads elsewhere in the county, such as Broadheath near Altrincham. Scientific analysis of such material can provide an insight into the natural environment before the road was laid.

Excavated section of the Roman road at the Three Sisters in Ellesmere Park, Eccles (courtesy of WAS)

The First Excavations: 1982-4

Location of trenches excavated in the 1980s

The first opportunity to explore Wigan's Roman past under modern archaeological conditions was provided by a series of excavations carried out during the 1980s by GMAU. In 1982-3, three trenches were excavated between the top of The Wiend and Millgate, close to the summit of the hill on which the historic core of the town lies. In 1984, following the demolition of surrounding buildings, a fourth trench was excavated closer to Millgate, on the site that was to be developed as the Children's Library.

Excavations at the Wiend (courtesy of GMAU)

It became clear during these excavations that most archaeological remains on the higher ground in the northern part of the site had been destroyed by later development, although Roman levels survived to the south, preserved beneath overburden that was up to 2m thick. The remains of foundation trenches for large wooden sleeper beams and floor joists were discovered, providing good evidence for Roman timber buildings. Whilst the entire footprint of any one building was not exposed, it was calculated that they probably measured some 20m long and 8m wide, and it was thought that they may have had an open-end or loading bay. Several hearths that seemed to have been used for iron-working were also discovered, although these appeared to be of a slightly later date, having been put into use following the demolition of the timber buildings. However, there were few other physical remains that could be associated with the hearths, making it difficult to establish the true character of this Roman activity.

Excavations in 1984 on the site of the Children's Library (courtesy of GMAU)

The remains of a Roman iron-working hearth excavated at The Wiend in 1983 (courtesy of GMAU)

After assessing the evidence available, the excavators concluded that they had probably found the remains of Roman workshops or warehouses, which dated to between the late first and mid-second centuries AD. Comparable remains were excavated at Walton-le-Dale in the early 1980s, where large timber buildings and craft-working hearths were interpreted as the remnants of a Roman industrial site and military supply depot. Similarly, excavations at Wilderspool during the 1970s yielded evidence that was also thought to be the remains of a Roman industrial settlement. Against this background, it did not seem unreasonable to suggest that Wigan may also have been an industrial centre, where goods required by the Roman military were manufactured. However, despite the convincing evidence provided by these excavations for a Roman settlement at Wigan, many questions remained unanswered.

Excavations in 1984 on the site of the Children's Library (courtesy of GMAU)

The Joint Service Centre: 2008

Further archaeological investigation of the site was carried out in 2008 by Oxford Archaeology North (OA North) prior to the construction of the Joint Service Centre. This allowed for the thorough examination of a larger area than had been available in the 1980s, and provided an opportunity to build upon the findings from the previous excavations.

A view of part of the 2008 excavation site

The earliest remains to be found included the western end of a Roman timber building that had also been partly exposed during the 1980s. By combining the data gathered from the two excavations it has been possible to trace the footprint of at least part of the building, whilst dating evidence provided by fragments of pottery recovered from the excavated building indicated that it had probably been built during the late first century AD. The size and layout of the building closely resembled a typical barrack block used by the Roman army in Britain during this period.

Plan of the foundation trenches of the possible barrack

Aerial view of the Roman fort at Castleshaw (courtesy of GMAU)

Crucially, the presence of such barracks would strongly suggest that the excavation area lay within the footprint of a Roman fort. This allows an alternative interpretation of Roman Wigan to be put forward.

Roman forts were normally constructed to a standard layout, taking a rectangular form with a gateway built into each side. They varied in size, although the majority covered an area of 1.4 - 2.4ha (3.5 - 6 acres), and were designed to house a unit of 500 or 1000 troops. Those constructed in Britain during the late first century were usually built in timber, with a palisade on top of earthen banks, surrounded by a series of defensive ditches. Many, though, were later rebuilt in stone.

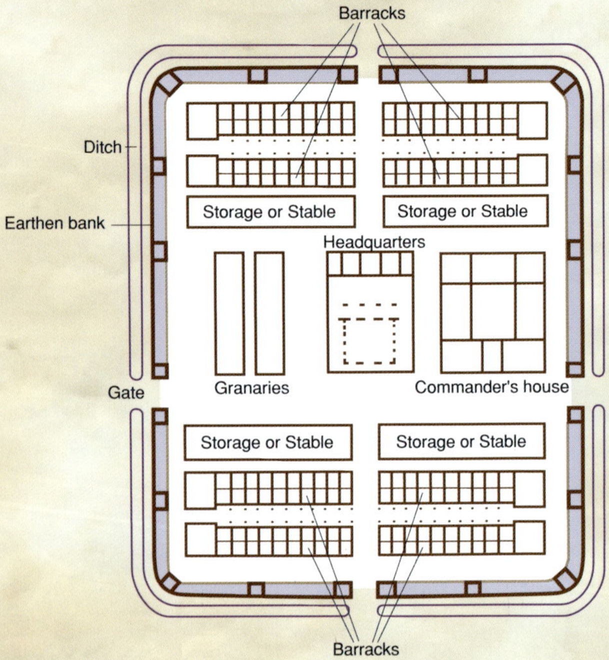

Standard layout of a Roman fort

The central part of a Roman fort was occupied by the most important buildings, such as the headquarters (*principia*), the commanding officer's house (*praetorium*) and the granaries (*horrea*), with soldiers' barracks (*centuriae*) and workshops situated to the front and rear.

Whatever the exact function of the building excavated in 2008, it appeared to have been demolished in the early second century, and the site was abandoned for a short while, before a series of iron-working hearths was constructed. The remains of two of these hearths were discovered, together with lumps of metalworking debris. Detailed examination of this material concluded that it derived from iron smithing, implying that the hearths had been used by blacksmiths.

Remains of an iron-working hearth excavated in 2008

As had been the case in the 1980s, the excavation in 2008 provided no evidence for any human activity on the site during the third or fourth century. This suggests that it had not been occupied during the late Roman period.

The Grand Arcade: 2004-5

The excavation on the site of the Joint Service Centre followed on from a large archaeological investigation that was carried out in advance of construction work for the Grand Arcade Shopping Development, on the opposite side of Millgate. This work was undertaken by OA North in 2004-5, and in the first instance involved the excavation of 36 trial trenches. These were targeted on parts of the site that were considered from desk-based research to have some potential to contain archaeological remains.

The trial trenches showed that whilst archaeological levels had been destroyed by nineteenth- and twentieth-century development over large parts of the site, some important buried remains did survive *in-situ*. Two areas in particular merited further investigation: a narrow

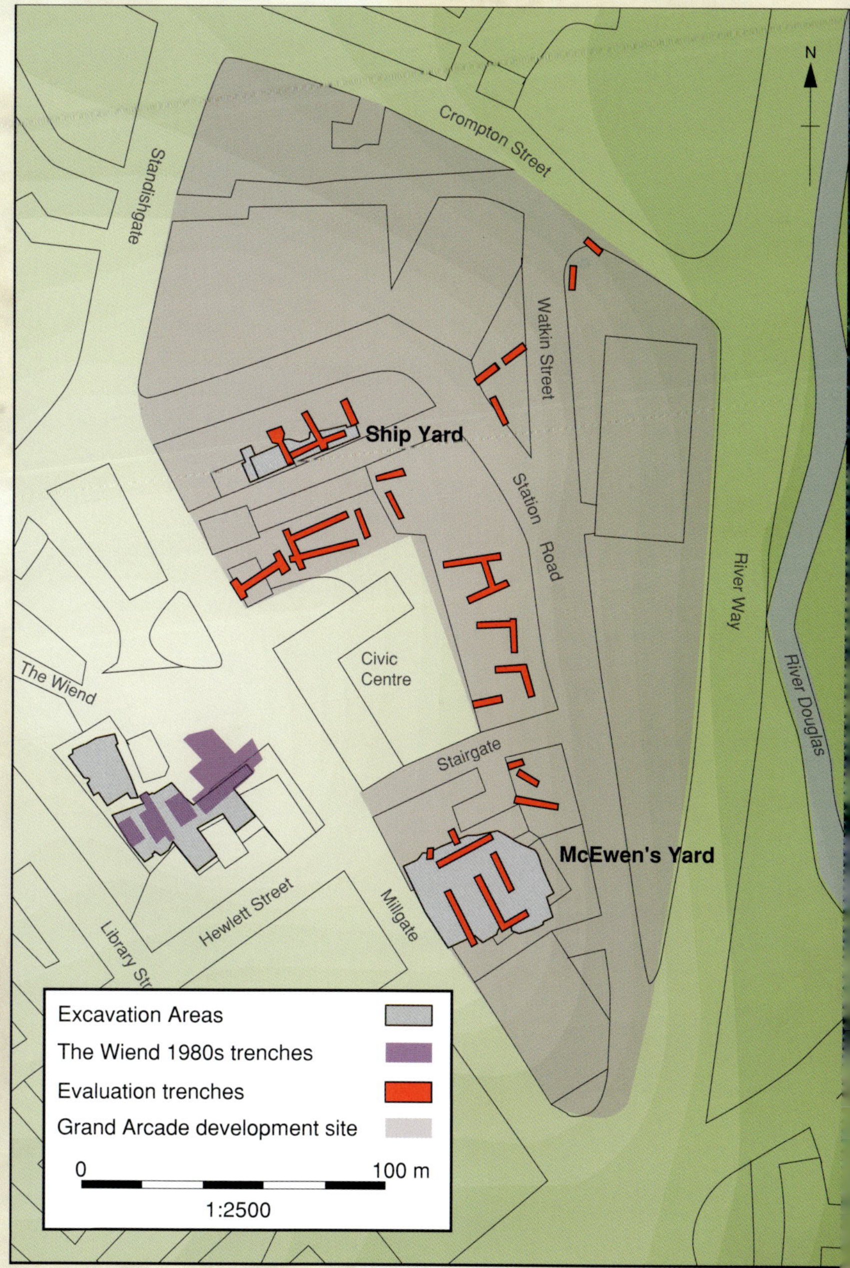

Plan of the trial trenches and excavation areas, showing the street layout prior to development

strip across the former Ship Yard, where significant medieval and post-medieval deposits had been identified; and a larger area to the south, incorporating the former Powell's Yard and McEwen's Yard, where more medieval remains and a small Roman hearth had been discovered.

Although no Roman deposits had been identified initially at Ship Yard, further excavation revealed two ditches, which were aligned east/west and set approximately 3.5m apart. Both had broad V-shaped profiles, suggesting a military origin. Their original upper parts had almost certainly been planed off by later development, as they only survived to a maximum depth of 0.5m. One of these ditches was waterlogged, providing a suitable environment for the preservation of organic material, including abundant fragments of wood. These were mostly small twigs, but also included a few short pieces of planks and numerous wooden pegs.

Excavation at Ship Yard, showing one of the Roman ditches (courtesy of GMAU)

The wooden pegs were all of oak, and were typical of those used by the Roman army for pitching tents. Most of the pegs were around 300mm long and around 40mm wide, although a few examples measured up to 420mm long. It is possible that the two lengths served different purposes, with the short examples being used for pegging the walls of the tent to the ground, and the longer ones for securing guy ropes. Fragments of a large storage jar that dated to the late first or second century were also found in the ditch.

Fragments of a large storage jar, found in a ditch at Ship Yard

The excavated remains at Ship Yard were certainly consistent with the use of the site by the Roman military. It is possible that the ditches had formed part of the defences for a fort or a temporary camp, which may have been established when the army first arrived at Wigan in the late first century, although there was insufficient evidence to be certain.

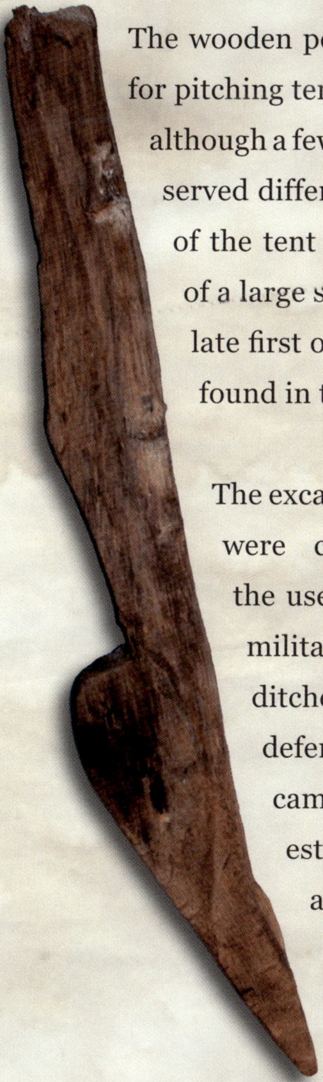

Roman wooden tent peg

More remarkable remains were excavated to the south, in the area of McEwen's Yard, where the foundations of a large and clearly very important building were discovered, together with many other Roman features. The surviving remains were sufficient to demonstrate that the building measured 36m long with a maximum width of 18m, and had been of stone construction with a tiled roof. It contained nine or ten rooms of different sizes, and had a colonnaded portico on the northern side, which presumably formed the main entrance.

Some of the uncovered hypocaust pilae

Laid directly onto the natural bedrock in three of the rooms were regularly spaced stacks of square tiles, known as *pilae*. These would have supported a raised floor in each of the rooms, which provided a clear indication that they had contained a below-floor heating system, or *hypocaust*. Many of the *pilae* stacks had been reduced to only a few tiles in height, although one example survived to nine courses (0.56m). The ground-plan of this structure, and the presence of the *hypocaust*, leaves little doubt that it was a bath-house.

In the north of Britain, nearly all bath-houses were built by the Roman army, and can be divided into two broad types: elaborate baths associated with legionary fortresses; and the smaller structures built for the garrisons of auxiliary forts. Examples of the former type are restricted to the legionary fortresses at York and Chester, where some fragmentary remains can still be seen today, whilst numerous examples of the smaller type of bath-house are known. The use of bath-houses was not limited to military personnel, and they were available to anyone upon receipt of a small entrance fee, although regulations prevented men and women from bathing together. They were central to Roman life, providing a place for people to exercise, bathe, and to establish and maintain social contacts.

A reconstruction drawing by Graham Sumner, showing the interior of a bath-house

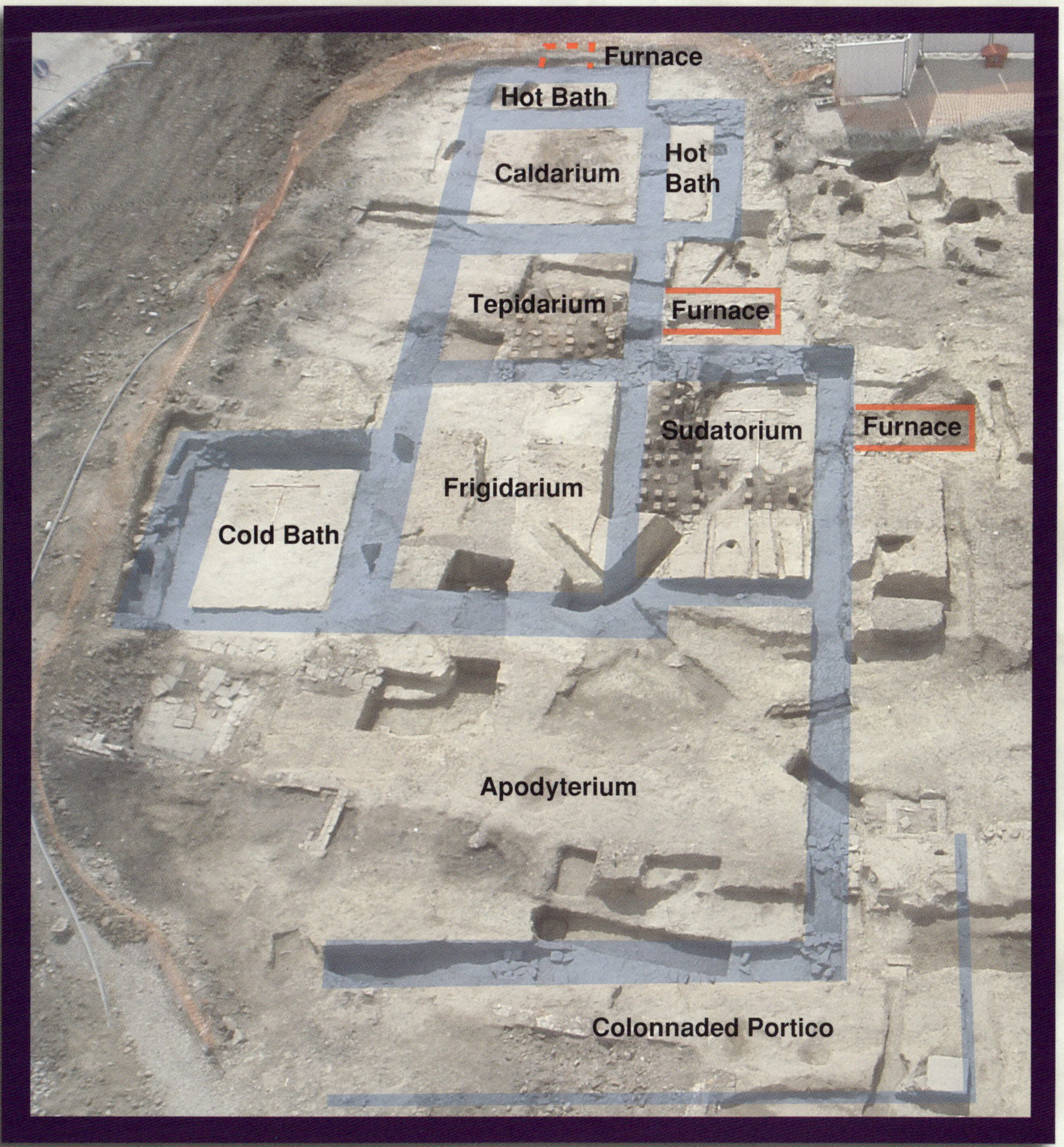

View of the excavated area, showing the footprint of the excavated bath-house

View of the excavated cold bath

Whilst they could vary considerably in size, all bath-houses contained the same essential features, including a suite of at least three principal rooms of differing temperature: the warm room (*tepidarium*); the hot room (*caldarium*); and the cold room (*frigidarium*), through which bathers would proceed in sequence. The *caldarium* was frequently equipped with small warm and hot baths, whilst a cold bath was often provided in the *frigidarium*. Many bath-houses would also have a changing room and/or exercise area (*apodyterium*), and a latrine.

After undressing in the *apodyterium*, the bather would proceed through the *frigidarium* to the *tepidarium*, where oil would be applied to the body. Sweating in the steam room (*sudatorium*) and *caldarium* would be followed by scraping the body with a *strigil* to remove sweat, oil and dirt, after which the bather would wash in a hot bath before returning to the *frigidarium* to cool down in a cold bath.

Rooms were heated by *hypocausts* beneath their floors, which were linked to external furnaces via arched tunnels that passed through the walls of the building. Hot smoke from the furnaces was drawn through the *hypocaust* and expelled outside via flues of hollow tiles that were set into the walls and roof of the bath-house.

Excavated hypocaust *furnace and the remains of an arched tunnel to allow the heat through the bath-house wall*

The hot water required in a bath-house was heated in bronze or lead boilers located directly above the hypocaust furnaces. Water was usually taken from a river, and was often carried along an aqueduct, such as those at Lincoln and Dorchester. However, whilst the bath-house at Wigan may have used the River Douglas as a source of water, it is difficult to see how an aqueduct could have been engineered to reach the site. It is conceivable that water was pumped from the river to supply the baths, since examples of force pumps are known from Roman Britain, and high-pressure water pipes of lead, earthenware or wood have been recorded at many sites. More likely, water may have been tapped from a natural spring, as at Bath in Somerset, which is one of the best surviving examples of a Roman bath-house in Europe. Interestingly, several nineteenth-century descriptions of Wigan mention natural springs impregnated with sulphur that rose to the surface in and around Wigan; some writers even referred to Wigan as 'New Harrogate', comparing it to the celebrated spa town in Yorkshire.

Excavating the pits to the west of the bath-house

Amongst the other Roman features exposed during the excavation were several square-shaped pits, which lay a short distance to the west of the bath-house. It is not known what function these pits had, although they may simply have been places to dump rubbish. Several small hearths, housed in a flimsy timber-framed structure to protect them from the elements, were also discovered during the excavation. Numerous droplets of molten lead were found around the hearths, suggesting that they had been used to make some of the fixtures and fittings for the bath-house.

Surprisingly, the bath-house was dismantled in the mid-second century, perhaps in order to reuse the masonry elsewhere, although the ceramic roof tiles were discarded in a heap. Just over one tonne of roof-tile fragments were recovered from the excavation, whilst only the vestiges of masonry walling survived.

Fragment of ceramic roof tile, with a nail hole

The dismantling of the bath-house appeared to coincide with a marked decline in Roman activity. A few fragments of third-century pottery were discovered, demonstrating that the area had not been abandoned entirely during the late Roman period, although there was no evidence for any buildings or any indication of the intensive use of the site.

Recording the vestiges of Roman masonry that had formed the south-western corner of the bath-house

THE FINDS

Fragments of a decorated samian ware bowl, dated c AD 80-100

Archaeological excavations of Roman sites often produce numerous artefacts, which commonly include fragments of pottery, glass, animal bones, iron and copper-alloy objects. However, surprisingly few organic and metallic artefacts were recovered from the excavations in Wigan, and these were all in very poor condition, reflecting the acidity of the soils in which they had been buried. Pottery is more resistant to such conditions, and more than 2000 fragments of Roman ceramic vessels were recovered from the Grand Arcade excavation alone. These included fragments of finely decorated red tableware vessels, known as samian ware, which was produced in vast quantities in Gaul and exported throughout the Roman Empire.

Other types of imported pottery found during the excavation included fragments of amphora. These large vessels were designed for storing and transporting oils and wine, and frequently had two handles, a narrow neck and a pointed base, allowing them to be stored upright by being embedded in sand or soft ground. All of the examples from Wigan were of a type that was produced in Spain as containers for olive oil, the importation of which was a significant trade in Roman Britain.

Part of a second-century black-burnished ware jar

Numerous fragments of black-burnished ware vessels, including bowls, dishes and jars, were also found. This functional type of pottery was intended for the storage,

Unguent pot

preparation and serving of foodstuffs. Black-burnished ware was produced on an industrial scale around Poole Harbour in Dorset, and is frequently discovered on Roman sites throughout Britain. A range of other functional types of domestic wares was also found, included grey wares and oxidised wares, some of which may have been produced locally. An unusual vessel discovered during the excavation was a small unguent pot, which will have contained an ointment used by visitors to the bath-house.

Over 200 fragments of Roman glass were also found at the site of the bath-house. Most of these fragments were very small, however, and probably represented only three actual vessels, together with part of a glass bangle. The glass vessels included a small bottle that may have been for cosmetics or bath oil, an unusual colourless beaker, and a delicate glass funnel. Several fragments of Roman window glass were also recovered, implying that the bath-house had been glazed.

Fragment of a small glass bottle

The largest single Roman object from the excavations was a large fragment of a moulded stone column, which had a maximum diameter of 0.40m. It had probably formed part of a colonnade at the northern end of the bath-house, and had been dumped in the *hypocaust* when the building was dismantled. It had been carved out of fine-grained sandstone, which had probably been quarried locally.

All of the artefacts, together with the complete archives generated from the excavations, have been deposited with the Museum of Wigan Life.

The fragment of Roman column

A reconstruction by Adam Parsons, showing the buildings typical of a Roman settlement

It is clear from the remarkable evidence gained from the recent excavations that Wigan was an important Roman settlement, and was almost certainly the place referred to as *Coccium* in the Antonine Itinerary. This probably comprised a military station and an associated settlement, which may have been inhabited by soldiers' families, craft-workers and tradesmen providing supplies and entertainment for troops when they were off duty. This type of settlement was known as a *vicus*, and frequently developed adjacent to a Roman fort. They were sometimes transitory sites, as the population followed an army unit when it was relocated.

A military station in Wigan may have been first established in the early AD 70s, when the Roman army embarked on a major campaign across the North West. It is possible that a temporary camp was constructed initially, where Roman soldiers were housed in leather tents, while a more substantial fort containing timber buildings was being constructed.

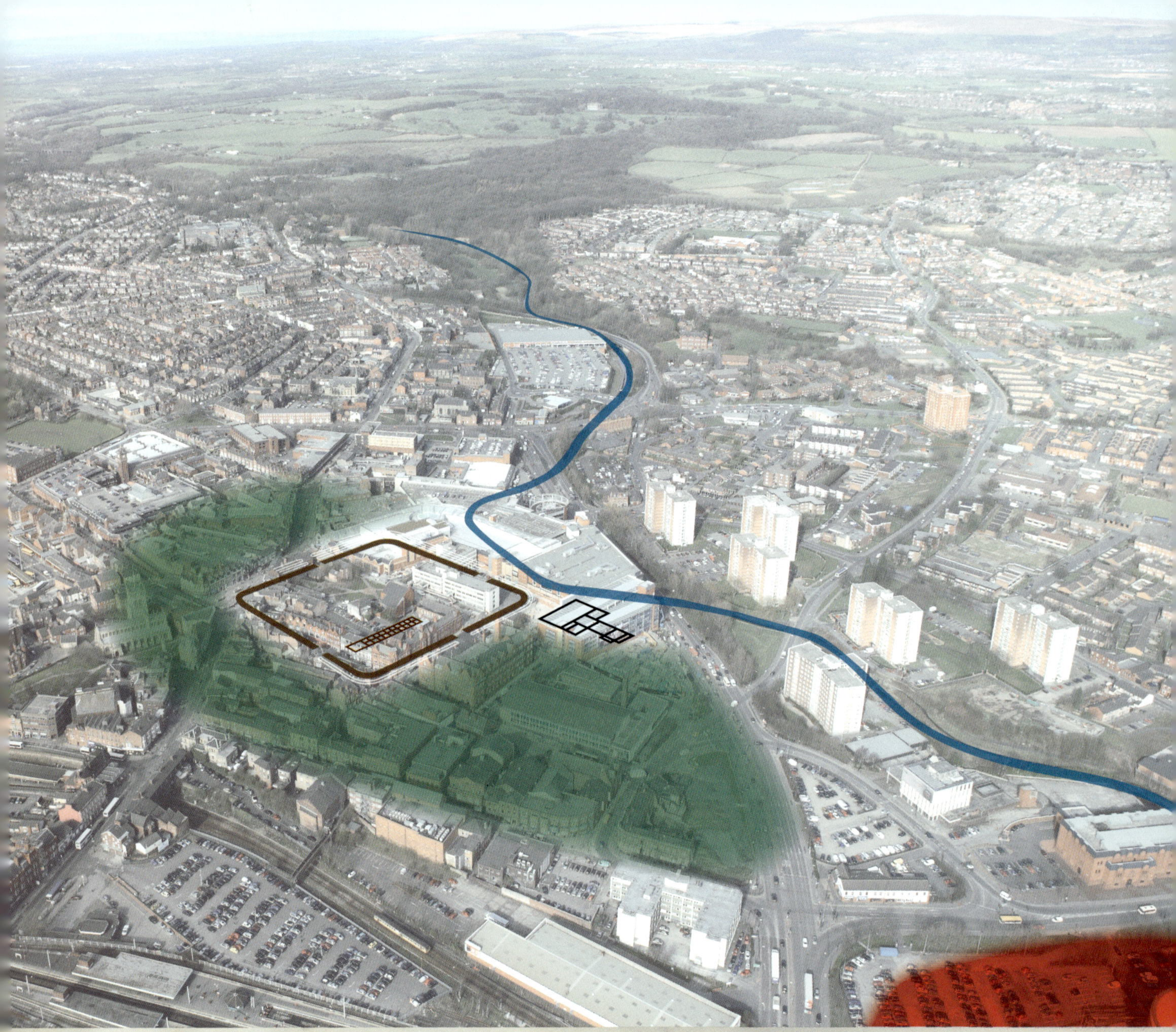

Speculative plan of Roman Wigan, superimposed on an aerial view of the modern town (© webbaviation)

If the timber building excavated at the Joint Service Centre has been interpreted correctly as a barrack block, it is likely that a Roman fort occupied the crest of the hill, taking advantage of the strategic position overlooking the River Douglas. The long axis of such a fort would probably have been orientated approximately east/west, with the centre perhaps lying in the vicinity of the present-day junction of The Wiend with Millgate. However, this is purely speculation and confirmation is dependent on future archaeological excavations, which may provide additional evidence and allow us to revise our interpretation of Roman Wigan further.

There is presently little evidence to show how large any associated settlement might have been, although its focus may have been to the south-east of the modern town centre, in the area between Millgate and King Street, where numerous Roman artefacts were found in the nineteenth century. The discovery of a cemetery near Darlington Street implies that the settlement did not extend beyond the bottom of Millgate, as Roman statute prohibited burials in residential areas.

Bath-houses were often sited some distance from other buildings, as the *hypocaust* furnaces represented a serious fire risk to timber buildings. The bath-house in Wigan was no exception, and probably lay on the eastern edge of the settlement. Excavation has shown that the bath-house had an interior area of 340m², which was somewhat larger than other bath-houses in the region, including those connected with the forts at Great Chesters and Carrawburgh on Hadrian's Wall. Both of these forts were garrisoned by cohorts of approximately 500 troops, and it is possible that a fort at Wigan may have been intended for a similar-sized regiment.

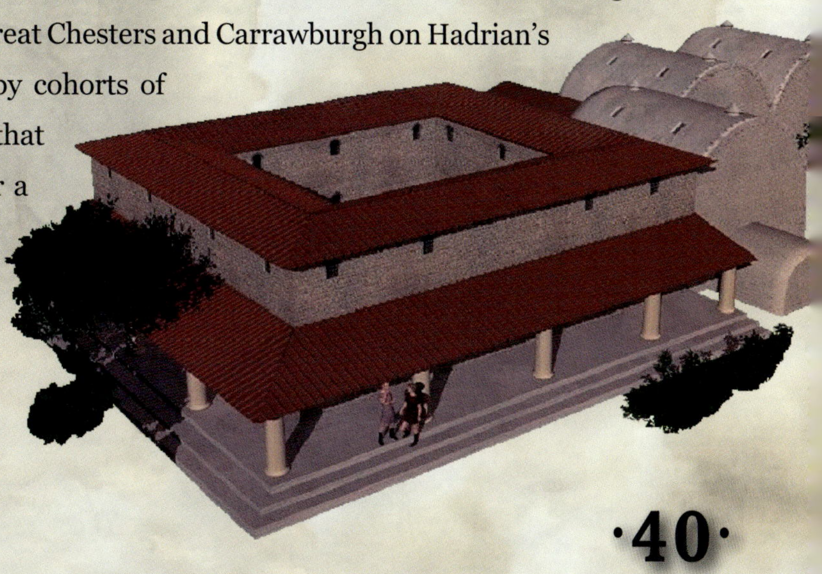

A computer-generated reconstruction of the bath-house by Dave Horrocks for WAS. The layout of the building is based on the excavated plan, whilst its appearance mirrors known examples of bath-houses in Europe

An illustration by Graham Sumner, providing a slightly different interpretation of how the bath-house may have looked

Whilst the excavation has provided evidence for the size, layout and date of the bath-house, the actual appearance of the building is a matter of interpretation. However, it will certainly have been an important landmark, which could probably have been seen from a considerable distance to the east, symbolising the power and influence of Roman rule.

Evidence provided from the excavations has demonstrated that Wigan was an important place between the later first century and *c* AD 160, when the bath-house was dismantled. There is little indication for Roman activity in the vicinity of Millgate thereafter, although third- and fourth-century coins have been discovered elsewhere in the town. This suggests that whilst the Roman army may have left Wigan, resulting in a substantial reduction in the size of the settlement, some occupation of the area nevertheless continued. The nature of occupation during this period is unknown, and whilst it is likely to have been based on subsistence agriculture, this can only be confirmed and clarified by future archaeological excavations.

THE PLANNING BACKGROUND

Aerial view of the Grand Arcade development in 2005 (courtesy of Wiganworld)

The recent excavations in Wigan were undertaken by OA North to satisfy planning conditions for the development of the Grand Arcade and the Joint Service Centre. Wigan Council attached these conditions to planning consent on the recommendation of GMAU, which also devised a specification for the scope of works required. GMAU in addition provided advice through the entire process from starting the initial evaluation trenching through to final publication.

The programme of archaeological works was intended to establish whether any important buried remains survived within the development sites, and to make a detailed and accurate record of any that were found to exist. This process is known as 'preservation by record' and it leads to the creation of a technical report and site archive, which in this instance has been deposited with Wigan Heritage Services. A selection of the artefacts from the excavations, together with some of the finds discovered by chance in the town, are on display in the Museum of Wigan Life on Library Street. This approach is in accordance with current national planning policies, which are set out in Planning Policy Statement PPS 5 *Planning for the Historic Environment*.

PPS 5 also stresses the importance of making the information generated from archaeological investigations publicly available and, where possible, to involve local communities in the data-gathering process. However, it is often difficult to engage the public during excavations of this nature, due largely to the rigorous health and safety requirements on construction sites,

Visitors on site during a public open day

although a public open day was held towards the end of the excavation at the Grand Arcade, which was attended by over 1000 people. Several school parties were also invited to visit the excavation, and numerous lectures have been delivered to local history and archaeology societies.

The site of the Roman bath-house has now been built over. However, the *hypocaust pilae* revealed during the excavation, together with the fragments of Roman masonry recovered from the excavated building, have been used in a reconstruction of a room in the bath-house. This can be seen in the public square to the rear of the Grand Arcade, and provides a rare physical reminder of Wigan's rich Roman heritage.

Reconstructed part of the bath-house to the rear of the Grand Arcade

GLOSSARY

AUXILIARY FORT: a medium-sized fort that provided a base for a **cohort** of auxiliary troops. Auxiliaries were recruited from the free provincial subjects of the empire, and formed the standing corps of the Roman Army.

COHORT: a military unit consisting of six *centuria* of 80 men, each commanded by a centurion.

GAUL: a region of Western Europe that incorporated present-day France, Luxembourg, Belgium, and parts of Switzerland, Northern Italy, Holland and the German Rhineland. Gaul came progressively under Roman rule during the second and first centuries BC.

ROUND BARROW: a prehistoric funerary monument that in its simplest form comprises a hemispherical mound of earth and/or stone that is raised over a burial in the centre, which may be placed in a stone chamber or a cut grave.

SAMIAN WARE: a distinctive type of plain and decorated fine tableware that was mass produced, and was distributed widely across the Roman Empire. Most of the samian found in Britain was made in factories in Gaul. Also known as *terra sigillata*.

SCHEDULED MONUMENT: an archaeological site that is recognised as being of national importance, and protected legally from development. Scheduled Monuments can range in date from the prehistoric period to the twentieth century, and can take many different forms, including buildings, earthworks or a cropmark in a field.

STRIGIL: a small, curved metal tool used by the ancient Greeks and Romans to scrape sweat, oil and dirt from the body.

FURTHER READING

- Brennand, M (ed), 2006 *The Archaeology of North West England. An Archaeological Research Framework for North West England: Volume 1. Resource Assessment,* CBA North West, **8** (18), Manchester
- Buxton, K, and Howard-Davis, C, 2000 *Bremetenacum: Excavations at Roman Ribchester, 1980, 1989-1990,* Lancaster Imprints **9**, Lancaster
- de la Bédoyère, G, 2001 *The Buildings of Roman Britain,* Stroud
- Jones, G C, and Price, J, 1985 Excavations at The Wiend, Wigan 1982-4, *The Greater Manchester Archaeological Journal,* **1**, 25-37
- Margary, I D, 1973 *Roman Roads in Britain,* 2nd edn, London
- Nevell, M, and Redhead, N (eds), 2005 *Mellor: Living on the Edge. A Regional Study of an Iron Age and Romano-British Upland Settlement,* Manchester
- Powell, P, 1998 *Wigan Town Centre Trail,* 2nd edn, Wigan
- Walker, J (ed), 1989 *Castleshaw: The Archaeology of a Roman Fortlet*, The Archaeology of Greater Manchester, **3**, Manchester
- Rook, T, 1992 *Roman Baths in Britain,* Princes Risborough
- Tindall, A S, 1983 Excavations in Wigan, 1982-3, *Greater Manchester Archaeological Unit Annual Report, 1982-3,* Manchester
- Tindall, A S, 1985 Wigan: The Development of the Town, *The Greater Manchester Archaeological Journal,* **1**, 19-23
- Shotter, D C A, 2004 *Romans and Britons in North-West England,* 3rd edn, Lancaster
- Watkin, W T, 1883 *Roman Lancashire,* Liverpool

Details of Wigan Archaeological Society's Roman Roads Project can be found at www.wiganarchsoc.co.uk
A huge volume of historical information on Wigan can be found at www.wiganworld.co.uk

Publications in The Greater Manchester Archaeological Journal, Greater Manchester's Past Revealed *series,* The Archaeology of Greater Manchester *series, and* The Heritage Atlas *series are available from GMAU. Other titles are available from: http://www.gmau.manchester.ac.uk/*

All of the artefacts, together with the complete archives generated from the excavations, have been deposited with Wigan Heritage Services, Wigan Leisure and Culture Trust.